MONSTERS, DINOSAURS AND BEASTS

Written by:
Stuart Kallen

Published by Abdo & Daughters, 6535 Cecilia Circle, Edina, Minnesota 55439.

Library bound edition distributed by Rockbottom Books, Pentagon Tower, P.O. Box 36036, Minneapolis, Minnesota 55435.

Library of Congress Number: 91-073061   ISBN: 1-56239-040-6

Cover Illustrations by: Tim Blough
Interiors by: Tim Blough

Edited by: Rosemary Wallner

TABLE OF CONTENTS

Dream Monsters..5

Ancient Terrors 6

Lizard Kings 10

Weird Science 12

Monsters of the Deep 15

    The Loch Ness Monster 16

    The Beast of 'Busco 19

    Kraken – The Monster Squid 20

Monsters Who Live on Land 24

    Abominable Snowmen...................................26

    Sasquatch or Bigfoot 29

Monsters and More Monsters 35

    The Beast of Le Gevaudan.............................36

    The Thunderbird 38

Monsters From Outer Space 43

Beasts Unburdened 46

Night time sets free a thousand dream monsters.

DREAM MONSTERS

Day ends and night brings darkness to the world. Now is the time for us to rest our bodies. Our dreams walk the pathway to morning. We must make the voyage through darkness, but we can not make it alone. For the night sets free a thousand creatures — freakish felines, disturbing dragons, maniac monsters, muttering mummies, and stupendous serpents. These half-bodied and disembodied monsters haunt the dreamworld and care nothing for logic or reason. In these night dreams, time stands still, floors dissolve into thin air, and beasts read our thoughts and laugh at our fears.

When we jump awake with heart-thumping terror, we know we have been somewhere. We know that we have traveled to the world of human imagination where monsters and beasts have always lived and always died. Since it is impossible to prove or disprove the existence of monsters, some may doubt that they are real. But those of us who have traveled to the far reaches of dreams and stood face to face with these freaks of nature never question and never doubt. We know.

ANCIENT TERRORS

Monsters have walked the earth since the beginning of time. When human imagination was born more than one million years ago, the earth was a place of terror and delight. Good hunting and easy times were mixed with cold, hunger, and want. Early humans could not fathom the mysteries of storms and sunshine, hunger and health, life and death. To better understand their desires and fears, primitive people gave faces and forms to their world. God and goddess images were dreamed up for the good and right things. Things that could be counted on.

But there were those other things too. Ugly, dark things that seemed inhuman and wrong; threatening, out-of-place, spooky, wild, and impossible things that lacked explanations. Primitive people gave these things the monster image. And there were no shortage of things to make people panic, cringe, and quake—strange shadows in the woods; odd shapes floating in lakes; wild creatures foaming at the mouth; crashing sounds in the night; huge paw prints of unknown beasts; horrible snakes, lizards, and insects — the catalog is endless. The tales of terror were passed down for thousands of years.

Monsters have walked the earth since
the beginning of time.

After countless generations, these creatures of the netherworld took on a life of their own.

Many primitive artists made cave paintings of natural objects like animals and humans. But in some places in the world, there are petroglyphs (cave paintings) of the most outrageous beasts of all—dinosaurs! How could these artists portray creatures that were extinct for sixty million years before humans walked the earth? Did ancient people stumble across the bones of dinosaurs sticking out of the sand? Or is science wrong? Did these beasts live longer than any of us believe? Are sea serpents real after all? Are the relatives of the dinosaurs still swimming in the deepest depths of our oceans? Are hairy mountain beasts living remnants of our distant relatives? Even if our ancestors only found the bones of dinosaurs, they still must have been alarmed. After all, they had no way of knowing that the gigantic animals were extinct. For all they knew, a 100-foot long,murderous green monster, could pop over the hill at any minute and eat them up like so many insects. That dread must have followed them every hour of their lives. And if the real dragons never showed up, wild exaggerations would be fashioned out of every shadow. It would have been little comfort to know that the whole earth was ruled for 230 million years by beasts as monstrous as anything the mind could invent. Which makes rational thought, reason, and imagination the exception on this planet. Monsters are the rule!

Primitive artists made cave paintings of natural objects like animals and humans.

LIZARD KINGS

In the 19th century, science proved the existence of dinosaurs. The word "dinosaur" translates from Latin to mean "terrible lizard" or "fearfully great lizard." Of course not all dinosaurs were terrible. There were hundreds of different kinds of dinosaurs, ranging from dog-sized right on up to monster-sized. But some dinosaurs were monsters. The most famous of them all is the Tyrannosaurus Rex or the "tyrant king" of lizard land. Any animal with sixty teeth, each over 18 inches long, would be considered a monster in any book. The T-Rex could eat more meat in one bite than three humans could eat in two months! Thank goodness they lived over 75 million years ago.

The dinosaurs were the original monsters from which we fashioned countless other terrors. Bits and pieces of these creatures twirled round in a kaleidoscope of patterns to give us sea serpents, dragons, gargoyles, and numerous other demons. Yet we've only known about the existence of dinosaurs for the past one hundred years. Why do we have thousands of years worth of legend and folklore based on dinosaurs?

Could it be that deep in our minds we remember
the terrifying sight of dinosaurs as seen through
the eyes of our earliest ancestors?

Dinosaurs were the original monsters.

WEIRD SCIENCE

Whatever the answers, human history is rich with all manner of monsters, beasts and brutes. There are, of course, living animals that really seem to be monsters. Animals like hammerhead sharks, vampire bats, tarantulas, rattlesnakes, and crocodiles would certainly qualify as monsters. Another "monster" is the Komodo dragon, an enormous lizard that lives in Indonesia. This reptilian horror looks like a tiny lizard but is 23 feet long and weighs over 400 pounds. These living dragons eat anything they can catch, including humans. And they're fast.

These and other brutes have been captured, documented, and photographed. But there is a whole world of monsters that have been seen but not caught. They've panicked people, but no one has been able to prove or disprove their existence. These are the monsters of nightmares, whether sleeping or awake. The beasts that have haunted and terrorized humans and won't go away. The monsters that haunt the oceans, lakes, mountains, and forests. Where wild things roam, so does the unknown.

*The Komodo dragon is an enormous lizard
that lives in Indonesia.*

*Underwater creatures have remained a
mystery to modern man.*

MONSTERS OF THE DEEP

The most mysterious and unexplored place on the earth is the ocean. Humans have skimmed its surface for centuries, but until recently, it has been humanly impossible to investigate the ocean's inky depths. Even in modern times, very little of the ocean has been truly explored. Some lakes are so deep that they too have remained veiled to human eyes. Parting that veil is not easy. Expensive equipment, skilled divers, and large crews are necessary to probe the deepest depths. That is why there are so many underwater creatures that have remained a mystery, even in modern times.

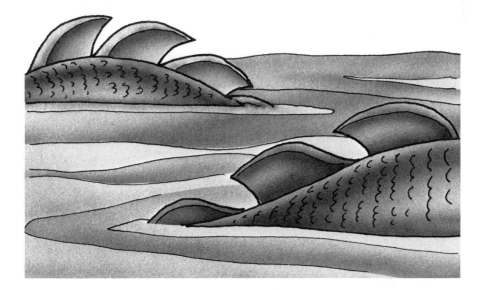

THE LOCH NESS MONSTER

The most famous water beast is the Loch Ness Monster, known lovingly as "Nessy." Nessy has been spotted hundreds of times in Loch (Lake) Ness in Scotland. Nessy looks like a plesiosaur, which is a kind of dinosaur. All in all, Nessy seems very mild mannered — not a monster at all, except in size. She's been filmed and photographed (or so we're led to believe) by American, Japanese, and English news crews. There is even a Scottish society called the Loch Ness Phenomenon Investigation Bureau that documents all Nessy sightings.

Monsters have been thought to live in Loch Ness since the Middle Ages. The Nessy craze got its start in 1933 when over 30 people independently recorded seeing something huge and reptilian swimming serenely in the Loch. Since then, sightings, investigations, and countless tourists have created an uproar at the once peaceful Loch Ness. Some believe that Nessy is a direct relative of the ancient dinosaurs. The mystery grows as Nessy hides out in the 1,000-foot depths of Loch Ness and feeds on its huge supply of fish.

*The Loch Ness Monster lives in
Loch (Lake) Ness in Scotland.*

While the Scottish serpent in Loch Ness is a world-famous monster, America also has its share of mysterious water creatures. Many American monsters were first mentioned in Native American legends and were later spotted by white settlers. One of these beasts is a serpent the size of a railroad car that was spotted in the White River in Arkansas. The White River Monster was last sighted in 1971. A variety of serpents have been seen at different times in Lake Champlain and Silver Lake in New York, Lake Payette in Idaho, Flathead Lake in Montana, Chesapeake Bay in Maryland, and Okanagan Lake in British Columbia, Canada.

THE BEAST OF 'BUSCO

A pond in Churubusco, Indiana, is the home of a giant turtle by the name of Oscar, known more ominously as the "Beast of 'Busco." In 1948, the owner of the pond noticed fish bones floating on the water. He also noticed that ducks resting on the pond would sometimes disappear, leaving nothing behind but floating feathers. The cause of these mysteries was Oscar, a giant snapping turtle. The largest snapping turtles can weigh up to 200 pounds and break broomsticks with their horned jaws. But the people in Churubusco said this turtle was bigger. Much bigger. Oscar was as big as a pickup truck.

A turtle hunt was organized, and a group of local men fished the pond with nets, traps, and hooks. They were unsuccessful. The farmer who owned the pond studied Oscar's habits and one day when the tremendous turtle was napping, the farmer slipped a chain around his middle. The chain was attached to four strong horses and the farmer tried to pull Oscar from the pond. The horses pulled and the turtle dug his claws into the mud. After 15 grueling minutes, the chain broke and Oscar disappeared, never to be seen again. Some say he died from the fight, others say he went into hiding. No one knows, but turtles can live a very long time and they are very patient. Maybe Oscar is just waiting for people to forget about him.

KRAKEN - THE MONSTER SQUID

A ship is sailing on calm seas through the 17 century South American sun. The first mate is keeping watch when he sees an island appear in the distance. He is puzzled because his maps do not show any islands in the area. As the ship approaches the island, the island begins to move. The sailor screams when he realizes that what he is seeing is not an island at all, but Kraken, a giant sea monster. Suddenly, Kraken becomes a twisting, writhing death monger and the ship his helpless prey. Eight 50-foot-long tentacles grab the ship. Kraken jams it into his monstrous, gaping mouth. The colossal squid dives to the ocean floor taking the wreckage of the splintered boat with it. The surface returns to calm as a few bubbles rise up from the dying men and their

Kraken — the monster squid.

doomed ship. Hours later, Kraken floats calmly on the waves, waiting for his next victim.

So goes the sailors' legend of Kraken. In the 18th century, sailors from the four corners of the earth told stories about the beast. In 1802, Denys de Montfort, a French naturalist, wrote a book of stories he had heard from American whalers about the gigantic, many-armed beast. De Montfort concluded that there were two different kinds of monsters: a giant squid and a giant octopus. One whaling captain told de Montfort that on the shore he had found an arm from a mammoth squid that was 45 feet long! De Montfort's book was met with ridicule and scorn. People called de Montfort a liar and a scoundrel. In 1820, he died penniless in Paris, a broken man. Still, no one ever disproved the legends of Kraken.

In 1886, Dr. De Witt Webb discovered and photographed a 10,000-pound octopus washed up on the shore in St. Augustine, Florida. The torpedo-shaped carcass had tentacles 32 feet long. The entire body was over 70 feet in length. The largest octopus ever discovered until that time weighed only 125 pounds. Reports and specimens of this startling find were sent to the Smithsonian Institution in Washington, D.C. Unfortunately, a storm washed the monster into the sea before it could be completely examined. The largest octopus ever found had disappeared forever.

In 1957, an ocean scientist named F. G. Wood re-examined the specimens and photographs that Dr. Webb had taken. Wood concluded that the monstrous octopus could very well indeed be a reality. De Montfort's Kraken and the giant octopus of St. Augustine could be relatives of the same animal. People had also sighted huge squids in Denmark in 1853 and in Newfoundland in 1863 and 1870. Perhaps de Montfort knew what he was talking about after all. Whatever the case, Kraken and his relatives remain a mystery to this day.

MONSTERS WHO LIVE ON LAND

Sightings of giant sea monsters terrorize sailors, fishermen, and ocean explorers. But most people never venture that far out onto the wild blue sea. Most landlubbers scoff at the wild tales sailors tell. But these are the same people who are jittery and frightened in the woods at night. It seems that more monsters lurk on land than in the ocean, as this old sailor's poem testifies:

> "Terrors of the deep
> cause sailors to lose sleep.
> But the terrors of the land
> haunt each and every man."

So, even if you're not a sailor, watch out! There may be a monster lurking in a field, forest, or mountaintop near you.

The abominable snowman lives in the Himalayan Mountains.

ABOMINABLE SNOWMEN

"Abominable" is a hard word to say, but the Abominable Snowman is even harder to find. And while "abominable" means horrifying or hateful, most people say the Abominable Snowman is mild mannered and shy. But there is more than one Abominable Snowman, and what he is called depends on where he lives. In the Himalayan Mountains of Tibet, the Abominable Snowman is called the Yeti. In the Canadian Rockies of British Columbia, he is known as Sasquatch. In the American Pacific Northwest, he is called Bigfoot. Other American relatives are the Skunk Ape of the Florida Everglades and Momo the Missouri Monster. But whatever the huge, hairy, humanoid mountain beast is called, he seems to be a member of a large and far-flung clan.

As thousands of sightings are recorded worldwide, a picture begins to emerge of the Abominable Snowman. He seems to come in three sizes: large, extra-large, and huge. He always walks upright like a human, but his body is covered with a thick, dark fur. His huge footprints have been photographed on nearly every mountain range in the world. The Abominable Snowman has been described at various times as being half-man/half-ape, of possessing supernatural intelligence, and of being extremely elusive. And he seems to be a gentle creature, monsterized by humans who cannot conceive of such an animal.

The existence of the Himalayan Yeti is never doubted by the Sherpa people who live in Tibet. They talk about the Yeti as they would any other animal. They say he lives in the deep forest thickets in the Himalayan forest and gets around by walking on all fours, or by swinging from tree to tree. Sometimes, he ventures into the open where mountaineers glimpse him walking with a rolling gait. The Sherpas say the Yeti is looking for a certain kind of moss when he appears in the open. The Yeti was first spotted by Westerners in 1925. N.A. Tombazi, a Greek photographer, saw what he thought was a Yeti walking across a snowfield. The Yeti's footprints were photographed in 1951 by Eric Shipton, a mountaineer. While the photographs became world famous, some doubted that they belonged to the Yeti. The existence of the Yeti is still a mystery to scientists.

Bigfoot or sasquatch has been seen hundreds of times and photographed at least once.

SASQUATCH OR BIGFOOT

The best proof of a real-life Abominable Snowman comes from the mountains of North America. The first European settlers in Oregon, Washington, and British Columbia were warned by local tribes of a strange wild man known as Sasquatch. Also known as Bigfoot, this creature has feet over 14 inches long, and likes to kidnap unsuspecting travelers. Bigfoot has been seen hundreds of times and photographed at least once.

In 1924, logger Albert Ostman, decided to look for a lost gold mine at the head of the Toba Inlet in British Columbia. An old Native American boatman told him that huge hairy beings lived in the mountains by the abandoned mine. Ostman ignored the man and started out on foot with his rifle, food, and sleeping bag. After a week's hike, Ostman settled down in a beautiful spot between two cypress trees. The camp spot was perfect, except that in the morning, Ostman would wake up to find that his supplies had been disturbed and some of his food had been taken. One night Ostman took his rifle to bed with him, hoping to surprise the food thief.

In the middle of the night, Ostman was awakened when his sleeping bag was picked up by the top. As Ostman struggled in the dark bag, he felt himself being transported as if on horseback. After hours in the stuffy, dark sleeping bag, Ostman was dropped amid a strange chatter he could not understand. He struggled out of his bag and saw four Sasquatch talking and gesturing to each other. The Sasquatch did not harm Ostman, but they seemed intent on keeping him. The Sasquatch seemed to be a family of an adult male, an adult female, a younger male, and a younger female. Ostman described them:

"The young fellow might have been 18 years old, about seven feet tall, and might weigh 300 pounds. He had wide jaws, narrow forehead and hair about six inches long. The old lady was about 50 years old, and weighed at least 600 pounds. She was over seven feet tall. She had very wide hips and a goose-like walk. She was not built for beauty or speed. The man's eyeteeth were longer than the rest of his teeth but not quite tusks. He must have been over eight feet tall. He had a big barrel chest, a big hump on his back and powerful shoulders.

His biceps were enormous. His arms were longer than common people have and his hands were wide and hollow like a scoop. His fingernails were like chisels. The only place he had no hair was on his palms, the soles of his feet, and the eyelids and nose."

After six days in such company, Ostman escaped by firing his rifle in the air and scaring the Sasquatch. Ostman did not tell of his encounter until 1955, because he was afraid he might be labeled as insane.

On July 16, 1918, the *Seattle Times* gave an account of "Mountain Devils" attacking a prospector near Mount St. Helens. The devils were said to be members of a local race with magical powers and the gift of invisibility-at-will.

In 1940, the Chapman family of Ruby Creek, British Columbia, was approached by an eight-foot-tall, hairy male creature who caused them to flee their home. He left behind 16-inch footprints and overturned a barrel of salted fish.

In 1969, near Bossburgh, Washington, a half-mile trail of 18-inch footprints was found. The 1,089 footprints walked easily over many obstacles including a four-foot-high fence.

The most incredible sighting was on October 20, 1967, when Roger Patterson filmed a Sasquatch in Bluff Creek, California. The film shows a hairy, man-like creature walking in full view of the camera. Experts who have examined the film found no evidence of fakery, even though it was shot in a place called Bluff Creek.

Perhaps the strangest Bigfoot story comes from a diary written in 1888 by Grandfather Wyatt, a Tennessee woodsman. Wyatt wrote that the local Native Americans had been in contact with strange, hairy beings that they called "crazy bears." The Native Americans claimed that they were brought down to earth from time to time by spacemen in what we would call UFO's. The spacemen were described as wearing silver, glittering outfits. Wyatt said in his diary that the spacemen were experimenting with stocking the earth with animals that they most liked to eat!

Bigfoot is a hairy man-like creature.

MONSTERS AND MORE MONSTERS

Bigfoot and his relatives are the ultimate half-man/half-monkey beasts. But history reveals tales of other monsters that resemble everything from giant earthworms to monstrous birds. There are even monsters that are a combination of other animals. The Dragon of Ishtar Gate has the head of a snake, the body of a lizard, the back feet of a bird, and the front feet of a cat!

A snake 131 feet long was photographed in 1949 in Brazil. The picture of the giant reptile was printed in a local newspaper. In Australia, people search for a creature called a bunyip. The bunyip has a large dog-like body equipped with fins for swimming. In the mid-19th century, bunyip hunting was a favorite pastime. An Australian expression that means "why try to do the impossible?" is "Why search for a bunyip?"

History reveals monsters that resemble everything from giant earthworms to monstrous birds.

THE BEAST OF LE GEVAUDAN

A child-killing beast terrified the French town of Le Gevaudan from 1764 to 1767. Known as the Beast of Le Gevaudan, this fantastic creature walked on two legs like a man, but was covered with short red hair and had a pig-like snout. It was as big as a donkey, and had short ears and a tail. The beast would attack children who were tending sheep and cattle in isolated mountain pastures.

Frightened peasants begged the king to kill the beast. A company of soldiers claimed to have killed it in February 1765, and the next spring children went back to tending their flocks in the mountains. The beast struck again, however, and the killings continued. The king had lost interest in the problems of Le Gevaudan, and several nearby villages were abandoned in fear. Finally in June 1767, a hunting party of noblemen surrounded the beast in a patch of woods. Jean Chastel, one of the hunters, killed the beast with two silver bullets.

The child killing Beast of Le Gevaudan.

The carcass of the terrible monster was carried from town to town in order to calm the peasants. The beast was buried, and today tourists are shown the spot where Jean Chastel sent the monster to its death. Some people today think that the beast was a rabid wolf, others think it was a werewolf. No one knows for sure, but during its three-year reign of terror, the beast is believed to have killed dozens of children.

THE THUNDERBIRD

To some, nothing is more terrifying than the idea of a mammoth bird swooping down out of the sky and carrying off a human like a hawk carries off a mouse. Ancient Middle Eastern mythology tells of Sindbad the Sailor and his encounter with a bird called a roc. The roc's eggs were so huge that they looked like the dome of a great building. The sky darkened when the roc flew overhead. The roc carried off elephants to feed its young. When Sindbad angered the roc, it dropped stones on his ships, sinking one of them. Explorer Marco Polo mentioned the roc in his writings, and tried to prove its existence.

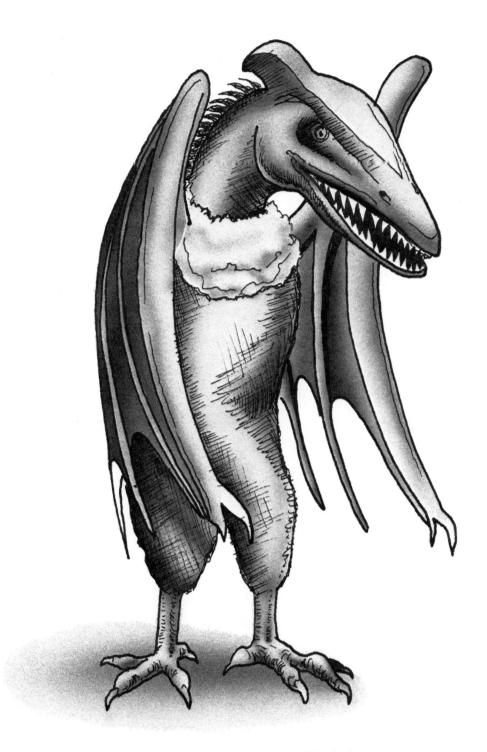

A terrifying creature called the roc,
darkened the sky when it flew overhead

Another bird from mythology is the thunderbird, which is mentioned in Native American legends. Some believe that the thunderbird is real and may exist today. The best story of a thunderbird sighting comes from Tombstone, Arizona. In 1886, a group of hunters claimed to have killed a thunderbird. They nailed it up on a barn with its wings outstretched. The men took a photograph of the bird-beast and, to give proof of its size, six men stood in front of it with their arms outstretched and their fingertips touching. This covered a distance of 36 feet! This is an astounding wingspan because the largest known living bird, the California condor, has a wingspan of eight feet.

The thunderbird's picture was printed in the *Tombstone Epitaph*, a local newspaper. Since then, the picture seems to have disappeared, although several researchers claim to have seen it. Another version of the thunderbird story holds that the creature was a featherless monster with razor-sharp teeth and a wingspan of 160 feet.

The Jersey Devil resembles a winged horse.

In 1972, the remains of a true flying monster, the pterodactyl, was unearthed in Big Bend National Park in Texas. This area is about 500 miles from Tombstone, Arizona. Some people think that the thunderbird killed in 1886 was a relative of the pterodactyl whose relatives have been hiding out in the desert for thousands of years.

In New Jersey, another flying monster called the Jersey Devil has been sighted over the years. This improbable critter is said to be the size of a large crane with a thick long neck, long back legs with cloven hooves, short front legs with paws, bat-like wings, and the head of a horse, dog, or ram. A drawing of the Jersey Devil, as seen by a couple from Gloucester, New Jersey, was printed in a Philadelphia newspaper in 1909.

MONSTERS FROM OUTER SPACE

Last but certainly not least, is the category of monsters from outer space. So many monsters of this type have been seen that reports of them could fill several books. Some people claim that the United States Air Force keeps in a freezer the bodies of several aliens who were killed when their space ship crashed in the desert in 1949. Believers say that if the reality of these space monsters leaked out, a worldwide panic would ensue.

Dozens of people claim to have been kidnapped by aliens. These aliens have been described as insect-like by some, and as "little green men" by others. In 1977, near Dover, Massachusetts, a man saw an alien with bright orange eyes, a tiny body, long fingers and toes, and peach-colored skin. Interest in the "Dover Demon" died rather rapidly. It seems that so many people had reported alien sightings that it wasn't big news anymore.

One person who did get famous from an alien sighting is Kathleen May who saw a fireball crash into the woods of Flatwoods, West Virginia, on September 12, 1952. May and several friends hurried to the crash sight and were confronted with a "fire-breathing monster, ten feet tall with a bright green body and a blood-red face. It looked worse than Frankenstein."

The witnesses said the Flatwoods monster wore a helmet or hood shaped like "the ace of spades." The eyes glowed in the dark, and the creature wore a long coat or robe. It moved among the group with a "bouncing floating motion." The group panicked and dashed madly away. May called the sheriff, who found nothing. Local people thought May and her friends were crazy. Despite the skeptical grumbling of the locals, the story caught on and accounts of the Flatwoods monster appeared in newspapers all over the country. May was invited to New York City to speak on a radio program about UFOs. The story was very popular, and for a short time, May was a celebrity.

The Flatwoods monster was a creature sighted in West Virginia in the 1950's.

No more was ever seen of the Flatwoods monster. Those who saw it were reluctant to talk about it further, fearing for their reputations and sanity. But the Flatwoods monster was the first major UFO-monster incident.

BEASTS UNBURDENED

The catalog of monsters is endless and the category huge. Some consider the true monsters to be evil humans who have caused more pain and misery throughout history than all other monsters combined. Some consider the monsters and beasts in this book to be nothing more than scientific curiosities or figments of the human imagination. Whatever the definition of real monsters, the telling of their stories will never cease. And maybe tonight while you're drifting off to sleep you'll see a monster or two. Are they real? Were they a fantasy? Only the monster knows for sure. Good night, and sweet dreams…